TISAX® Made Easy

AN EXPERT GUIDE FOR THE AUTOMOTIVE SUPPLIER INDUSTRY

Michael Kirsch

Copyright © 2023 Michael Kirsch

All rights reserved

The characters and events portrayed in this book are fictitious. Any similarity to real persons, living or dead, is coincidental and not intended by the author.

No part of this book may be reproduced, or stored in a retrieval system, or transmitted in any form or by any means, electronic, mechanical, photocopying, recording, or otherwise, without express written permission of the publisher.

TISAX® is a registered trademark of the ENX ASSOCIATION. The Author has no economic relationship with ENX. Mentioning the TISAX® trademark does not imply any statement by the ENX Association as to the suitability of the services advertised herein.

Cover design by: Michael Kirsch

Contents

Preface

In today's rapidly evolving digital landscape, information security and data protection have become critical concerns for organizations of all sizes and industries. With the increasing volume and sensitivity of digital information, it is essential to have robust security measures in place to protect against potential threats and breaches.

The TISAX® (Trusted Information Security Assessment Exchange) standard is a leading benchmark for assessing the information security and data protection capabilities of organizations. Developed by the Association of the Automotive Industry (VDA), TISAX® provides a common standard for assessing the security of information technology systems in the automotive industry.

This TISAX® implementation guide is designed to provide a comprehensive overview of the TISAX® standard and the TISAX® assessment process. It covers the key aspects of the TISAX® standard, including the background and history of TISAX®, the standard requirements, and the TISAX® assessment process. The guide also provides practical guidance on how to prepare for and successfully implement TISAX®, including how to conduct a gap analysis, develop a compliance roadmap, and identify and select the right tools and technologies.

This guide also provides practical advice and guidance on how to navigate the TISAX® assessment, including how to prepare for the assessment process, what to expect during the assessment, and how to manage non-conformities. The guide concludes with a discussion of how to maintain TISAX®

compliance over time, including tips and best practices for continuously monitoring and improving your organization's information security and data protection capabilities.

Whether you are just getting started with TISAX® or have already undergone an assessment, this guide provides the information and guidance you need to successfully implement and maintain TISAX® compliance. We hope that this guide will serve as a valuable resource for organizations looking to enhance their information security and data protection capabilities.

Chapter I: Introduction

A. Overview of TISAX®

TISAX® (Trusted Information Security Assessment Exchange) is a cybersecurity assessment framework that has been developed specifically for the German automotive industry. It provides a common evaluation and assessment framework for organizations operating in the sector and was created by the German Association of the Automotive Industry (VDA) to reduce the risk of cyber-attacks. The TISAX® framework is designed to help organizations demonstrate their commitment to cybersecurity and provide a standardized method for evaluating the security posture of companies operating in the automotive sector.

The automotive industry has become increasingly reliant on technology, with connected vehicles and other digital systems becoming more prevalent. As a result, cybersecurity has become a top priority for organizations in the sector, as cyber threats can compromise sensitive information, disrupt operations, and damage the reputation of companies. To address these threats, TISAX® provides a comprehensive and consistent method for evaluating the cybersecurity posture of organizations in the sector.

B. Importance of TISAX® compliance

Cybersecurity is a critical issue for organizations of all sizes and industries, and the automotive sector is no exception. With the increasing reliance on technology and the growing threat of cyber-attacks, it is more important than ever for organizations in the sector to take proactive measures to protect their sensitive information and operations. TISAX® compliance is a requirement for organizations operating in the German automotive sector and helps to reduce the risk of cyber-attacks by providing a comprehensive and consistent method for evaluating the security posture of companies.

TISAX® compliance helps organizations to build trust with their customers, partners, and stakeholders, as it demonstrates their commitment to cybersecurity. By complying with the TISAX® framework, organizations can maintain the confidentiality and integrity of sensitive information and protect their reputation. TISAX® also helps organizations to identify areas where they can improve their cybersecurity posture and provides a roadmap for ongoing improvement.

Firstly, TISAX® helps organizations to manage their cybersecurity risks and to improve their security posture. This is essential in today's world where cyber threats are increasing and the consequences of a security breach can be devastating. By complying with TISAX® standards, organizations can demonstrate to their partners and customers that they take information security seriously and that they are doing everything they can to protect sensitive information.

Secondly, TISAX® helps organizations to establish themselves as a trusted partner in the automotive supply chain. In the automotive sector, the exchange of sensitive information between organizations is common and the protection of this information is critical. TISAX® provides a common language and a set of best practices for managing information security, making it easier for organizations to work together and to establish trust.

Thirdly, TISAX® compliance can help organizations to increase their competitiveness. By complying with TISAX® standards, organizations can demonstrate to their partners and customers that they have a high level of information security, which can help them to win new business and to retain existing business.

Finally, TISAX® can help organizations to comply with legal and regulatory requirements. Information security is a complex area, and complying with all relevant laws and regulations can be a challenge. By complying with TISAX® standards, organizations can demonstrate that they are taking all necessary steps to protect sensitive information, and they can be confident that they are in compliance with the relevant laws and regulations.

In conclusion, TISAX® compliance is an important step for organizations in the automotive sector to manage their cybersecurity risks, establish themselves as trusted partners, increase their competitiveness, and comply with legal and regulatory requirements. By complying with TISAX® standards, organizations can demonstrate their commitment to information security and help to build a more secure and trustworthy automotive supply chain.

C. Objectives of the guide

The main objective of this guide is to provide a comprehensive and practical guide for organizations to implement TISAX® and achieve compliance. The guide covers all the key aspects of TISAX®, including the requirements, assessment process, implementation, and assessment. It is designed to help organizations understand the importance of TISAX® compliance and provide practical advice and best practices to help them achieve and maintain compliance.

This guide is intended for a wide range of stakeholders, including cybersecurity professionals, IT managers, business managers, and compliance managers. It provides a step-by-step approach to TISAX® implementation, making it easy for organizations to understand and comply with the TISAX® standards. The guide also includes real-world examples, case studies, and practical tips to help organizations achieve TISAX® compliance and maintain their cybersecurity posture.

The guide is structured in a logical and easy-to-follow manner and provides a detailed explanation of each aspect of TISAX®. The guide starts by providing an overview of TISAX® and its importance, and then moves on to cover the key elements of TISAX® compliance, including the assessment process, implementation, and assessment. The guide also covers the key aspects of TISAX® that organizations need to consider when preparing for and navigating the assessment process and provides practical tips and best practices to help organizations achieve TISAX® compliance.

The guide concludes by providing an overview of the key takeaways, future outlook, and final thoughts. The guide is intended to be a comprehensive and practical resource for organizations to implement TISAX® and achieve compliance and provides a wealth of information and best practices to help organizations navigate the TISAX® framework.

Chapter II: Understanding TISAX®

Chapter II of TISAX Made Easy focuses on providing a comprehensive understanding of the TISAX standard. The chapter begins with a background and history of TISAX, providing insight into the origins and evolution of the standard. It then goes on to discuss the standard requirements, outlining the key elements of TISAX that organizations must comply with.

The chapter also explores the TISAX assessment process, delving into the various stages of assessment, from preparation to the final report. This section provides a detailed overview of what organizations can expect during the assessment process, as well as key considerations to keep in mind.

Finally, the chapter concludes with a discussion of the types of TISAX assessments, highlighting the different types of assessments available and their specific requirements. Whether you are a small business or a large enterprise, this chapter provides a comprehensive understanding of TISAX and its requirements, helping you to prepare for implementation.

A. Background and history of TISAX®

The Trusted Information Security Assessment Exchange (TISAX®) was created to address the fragmented approach to cybersecurity assessments in the German automotive sector. Prior to TISAX®, each Original Equipment Manufacturer (OEM) had their own set of questions and performed their own audits on suppliers, resulting in inconsistent and non-standardized assessments. This made it challenging for suppliers to maintain compliance with multiple OEMs, as the results of one audit were not recognized by others.

To address this issue, the German Association of the Automotive Industry (VDA) developed TISAX® as a unified cybersecurity assessment framework. The framework is based on the ISO/IEC 27001 standard, which is widely recognized as a best practice for managing information security. TISAX® was created to help organizations in the automotive sector manage cybersecurity risks and improve their security posture by providing a standardized and consistent assessment process. The TISAX® framework is designed to help organizations understand the requirements for information security and implement the necessary measures to achieve compliance.

TISAX® assessments are performed by accredited assessors and are designed to evaluate an organization's security posture and identify areas for improvement. By participating in TISAX® assessments, organizations can demonstrate their commitment to information security and gain recognition for their efforts. This can help build trust with customers, partners, and other stakeholders, and can also lead to new business opportunities.

TISAX® has become a widely recognized and respected cybersecurity assessment framework in the German automotive sector, and it continues to evolve and improve to meet the changing needs of the industry. By participating in TISAX® assessments, organizations can stay ahead of the curve in terms of cybersecurity and ensure that their systems and processes are secure and up-to-date. This guide will provide a comprehensive overview of the TISAX® framework, including the requirements, assessment process, and key considerations for implementation and preparation for assessments.

B. *TISAX® Standard Requirements*

The TISAX® standard requires organizations to implement a comprehensive information security management system (ISMS) that covers all aspects of cybersecurity, including risk management, incident management, and access control. The TISAX® standard is designed to be flexible and scalable, so that it can be applied to organizations of all sizes, from small suppliers to large OEMs.

The TISAX® standard includes several key requirements, including:

Security Policy: Organizations must develop and implement a security policy that outlines the organization's commitment to cybersecurity. This policy should be communicated to all employees and stakeholders.

Risk Management: Organizations must implement a risk management process that includes regular assessments of the organization's cybersecurity posture, and the identification and management of risks.

Incident Management: Organizations must have a process in place for managing cybersecurity incidents, including the ability to detect, respond to, and recover from incidents.

Access Control: Organizations must implement appropriate access controls to protect sensitive information and systems from unauthorized access.

In addition to the key requirements outlined above, the TISAX® standard also includes specific requirements for prototype protection and data protection. Prototype protection is a critical aspect of information security in the automotive industry, as it ensures that valuable and confidential information is protected from theft, unauthorized access, and misuse. The TISAX® standard requires organizations to implement appropriate measures to protect prototypes, including physical and logical access controls, and data encryption.

Data protection is another important aspect of information security that is covered by the TISAX® standard. The standard requires organizations to implement measures to protect personal data, including customer data and employee data, from unauthorized access and misuse. This includes implementing technical and organizational measures to ensure the confidentiality, integrity, and availability of data, and adhering to relevant data protection laws and regulations.

In conclusion, the TISAX® standard is a comprehensive framework that covers all aspects of cybersecurity and information security, including risk management, incident management, access control, prototype protection, and data protection. Organizations that are looking to achieve TISAX® certification must implement the requirements outlined in the standard and undergo a rigorous assessment process to demonstrate their compliance. By implementing the TISAX® standard, organizations can improve their cybersecurity posture and reduce their risk of a breach, thereby protecting their valuable information and assets.

C. Understanding the TISAX® Assessment Process

The TISAX® assessment process is a comprehensive and systematic approach to managing information security and protecting sensitive data. The process not only helps organizations meet the TISAX® standard requirements, but also provides valuable insights into their current security posture, as well as opportunities for improvement.

The preparation phase is crucial for the success of the TISAX® assessment. Organizations need to familiarize themselves with the TISAX® standard requirements, understand the scope of the assessment, and plan for the implementation of the ISMS. This may involve mapping out the organization's current security posture, conducting a risk assessment, and developing a comprehensive ISMS.

Once the preparation phase is complete, organizations can move on to the implementation phase. This phase involves developing and documenting policies, procedures, and processes to meet the TISAX® standard requirements. Organizations may also need to train their employees and stakeholders on the ISMS and its requirements.

The assessment phase is where an independent auditor evaluates the organization's ISMS to ensure that it meets the TISAX® requirements. The auditor will review the organization's policies, procedures, and processes, as well as conduct on-site assessments to verify that the ISMS is being implemented effectively.

If any deficiencies are identified during the assessment, organizations need to address them in the remediation phase. This may involve making changes to the ISMS, implementing new controls, or updating policies and procedures. Organizations also need to demonstrate that they have addressed the deficiencies and implemented the recommended improvements.

The final step of the TISAX® assessment process is certification. Upon successful completion of the assessment, organizations can obtain TISAX® certification, which is a demonstration of their commitment to cybersecurity and their ability to manage cybersecurity risks effectively. This can help organizations build trust with their partners, suppliers, and customers, as well as increase their competitiveness in the market.

In conclusion, the TISAX® assessment process is an important tool for organizations looking to improve their cybersecurity posture and protect their sensitive information. By following the TISAX® process, organizations can benefit from a comprehensive and systematic approach to information security, and gain a competitive edge in the market.

D. Types of TISAX® Assessments

The TISAX® assessment framework offers two types of assessments, each designed to meet the specific needs and requirements of different organizations.

TISAX® Basic Assessment: This type of assessment is suitable for organizations that are just starting to implement an information security management system (ISMS). The TISAX® Basic Assessment focuses on the basic requirements of the TISAX® standard, including the implementation of a security policy, risk management processes, incident management processes, and access controls.

Organizations that undergo a TISAX® Basic Assessment will receive a report that outlines any areas of non-compliance with the TISAX® standard, along with recommendations for improvement. The assessment process is designed to be flexible and adaptable, allowing organizations to implement the ISMS at their own pace and to tailor their approach to meet their specific needs.

TISAX® Advanced Assessment: This type of assessment is suitable for organizations that have already implemented an ISMS and are looking to improve their security posture. The TISAX® Advanced Assessment focuses on the advanced requirements of the TISAX® standard, including the implementation of more sophisticated security controls, such as continuous monitoring, vulnerability management, and penetration testing.

Organizations that undergo a TISAX® Advanced Assessment will receive a more detailed report that provides a comprehensive assessment of their ISMS. The assessment process is designed to be rigorous, and organizations are expected to demonstrate a high level of compliance with the TISAX® standard.

Both the TISAX® Basic and Advanced Assessments are conducted by independent auditors who are trained and certified to evaluate the ISMS of organizations against the TISAX® standard. The assessments are designed to be rigorous and impartial, and the results are used to help organizations improve their security posture and better protect their sensitive information and systems.

In conclusion, the TISAX® assessment framework provides organizations with the tools and guidance they need to implement an effective ISMS, and the choice of a TISAX® Basic Assessment or TISAX® Advanced Assessment depends on the organization's specific needs and current security posture. Whether you are just starting to implement an ISMS or looking to improve your existing security posture, the TISAX® assessment framework can help you to manage your cybersecurity risks effectively.

Chapter III: Preparing for TISAX® Implementation

Implementing the TISAX® standard can be a complex and challenging process, but with proper preparation and planning, organizations can ensure a successful outcome. In this chapter, we will cover the key steps involved in preparing for TISAX® implementation, including conducting a gap analysis, developing a compliance roadmap, building a TISAX® implementation team, and identifying and selecting the right tools and technologies.

A. Conducting a gap analysis

The first step in the TISAX® implementation process is critical in ensuring the success of the overall assessment. A gap analysis is the foundation on which the implementation will be built and provides a clear picture of the organization's current information security management system (ISMS) and the areas that need improvement. It is essential to evaluate the ISMS against the TISAX® standard requirements to determine the extent of compliance and to prioritize the implementation efforts accordingly.

Conducting a gap analysis requires a thorough understanding of the TISAX® standard and its requirements. The standard is a comprehensive guide to information security management, and it is important to pay close attention to the areas that apply specifically to your organization. Organizations should also review their existing security policies, procedures, and controls and compare them to the TISAX® standard requirements. This will provide a clear understanding of what needs to be done to bring the ISMS into compliance with TISAX®.

Inviting key stakeholders, such as security professionals and business users, to participate in the gap analysis process is an important step in ensuring a comprehensive understanding of the organization's current security posture. This can help identify areas of risk and security weaknesses, and provide valuable insights into the areas that need improvement. The gap analysis process should involve a thorough examination of the organization's ISMS, including its security policies, procedures, and controls, to ensure that all requirements are met.

Once the gap analysis is complete, organizations can develop a comprehensive plan for the implementation of the ISMS. This may involve developing new policies, procedures, and controls, updating existing ones, and providing training to employees and stakeholders. The implementation process should be well-planned and managed to ensure that it is completed in a timely and cost-effective manner.

It is essential to remember that the implementation of the ISMS is not a one-time event but rather a continuous process of improvement. Organizations should regularly monitor and assess their ISMS to ensure that it remains effective and efficient. Regular assessments of the ISMS can also help identify areas for improvement, which can then be addressed through ongoing implementation efforts.

In conclusion, the gap analysis is an important step in the TISAX® implementation process. It provides organizations with a clear understanding of their current security posture and the areas that need improvement, and helps prioritize their implementation efforts. Organizations should be proactive in their approach to information security management, and continuously monitor and assess their ISMS to ensure that it remains effective and efficient. The TISAX® standard provides a comprehensive guide to information security management, and organizations that implement it effectively can benefit from increased security, improved risk management, and a competitive edge in the market.

B. Developing a compliance roadmap

Having a comprehensive compliance roadmap is critical for the success of your TISAX® implementation project. It provides a clear and concise plan for how you will address any gaps in your current ISMS and bring it into compliance with the TISAX® standard. The roadmap serves as a roadmap for your team, providing guidance and direction for each step of the implementation process, and ensuring that all stakeholders are aligned with the project goals and objectives.

The first step in developing your compliance roadmap is to prioritize the gaps identified during the gap analysis. This involves determining which gaps are the most critical to address, and which can be addressed at a later time. For example, you may need to prioritize gaps related to the protection of sensitive data, such as customer information, over gaps related to less critical systems or processes. This will help you focus your efforts on the most important areas and ensure that your ISMS meets the most critical TISAX® requirements as quickly as possible.

Once you have prioritized the gaps, you can begin developing the compliance roadmap. Start by defining the objectives and activities for each step in the implementation process. For example, one step may involve developing and documenting security policies and procedures, while another may involve implementing technical controls, such as firewalls and intrusion detection systems. Be sure to include milestones for each step, such as the completion of a policy or the implementation of a new control. This will help you track your progress and ensure that you are on track to meet your objectives.

The compliance roadmap should also outline the resources required to complete each step. This includes the number of staff members needed, the budget required, and any technology or tools that need to be procured. For example, you may need to hire additional staff members with specific security expertise, or purchase new security software to meet the TISAX® requirements. Be sure to include all of the resources required to complete each step, and allocate the budget and personnel needed to ensure that the implementation project is completed on time and within budget.

Once the compliance roadmap is complete, you should review it with key stakeholders, including your security team, business users, and management, to ensure that everyone is aligned with the project goals and objectives. This is also a good time to discuss any concerns or challenges that may arise during the implementation process, and to make any necessary changes to the roadmap.

In conclusion, developing a comprehensive compliance roadmap is an essential step in preparing for TISAX® implementation. It provides a clear and concise plan for how you will address gaps in your ISMS and bring it into compliance with the TISAX® standard, and ensures that all stakeholders are aligned with the project goals and objectives. By following a well-defined roadmap, you can ensure that your TISAX® implementation project is completed on time and within budget, and that your organization is fully prepared to meet the TISAX® requirements and protect sensitive data.

C. Building a TISAX® implementation team

The team should also include a security professional who is knowledgeable about information security and TISAX® requirements, as well as a business representative who can provide insight into the organization's business processes and requirements. This will ensure that the implementation process is aligned with the organization's business goals and objectives, and that the ISMS meets the needs of the business users.

In addition to the core TISAX® implementation team, you may also need to involve other individuals and departments in the implementation process, such as legal, human resources, and procurement, to ensure that all necessary approvals, processes, and resources are in place.

To effectively manage the TISAX® implementation project, it is important to establish clear roles and responsibilities for each team member. This will help to ensure that everyone knows what is expected of them, and that the project is completed on time and within budget.

Finally, to ensure that the TISAX® implementation project is successful, it is important to establish effective communication channels between the TISAX® implementation team and key stakeholders, such as senior management, business users, and security professionals. This will help to keep everyone informed of the project's progress, and ensure that any issues are identified and resolved quickly.

In conclusion, building a strong TISAX® implementation team is crucial to the success of the TISAX® implementation project. By bringing together a diverse group of stakeholders and establishing clear roles and responsibilities, you can ensure that your ISMS meets the requirements of the TISAX® standard, and that the implementation project is completed on time and within budget.

D. *Identifying and selecting the right tools and technologies*

Building an effective information security management system (ISMS) is critical for organizations that need to comply with the TISAX® standard. A key component of this process is selecting the right tools and technologies to support the ISMS. One of the most important technologies that organizations should consider is a security information and event management (SIEM) system.

A SIEM system provides real-time analysis of security alerts generated by network hardware and applications. It centralizes log data from various sources and provides a single view of the entire network, making it easier to identify and respond to security incidents. By using a SIEM system, organizations can more effectively detect and respond to security incidents, and meet the requirements of the TISAX® standard.

In addition to SIEM systems, organizations should also consider other security management tools, such as intrusion detection and prevention systems (IDPS), and vulnerability management tools. These tools can help organizations identify and remediate potential security threats before they become actual incidents.

When selecting tools and technologies to support their ISMS, organizations should also consider the specific requirements of the TISAX® standard. They should ensure that the tools and technologies they select are capable of supporting the reporting and monitoring requirements of the standard, as well as providing the level of security required by the organization.

Finally, it is important for organizations to consider the ease of use, cost, and compatibility with their existing infrastructure and processes when selecting tools and technologies. In many cases, organizations will need to invest in training and support to ensure that the tools and technologies are used effectively.

In conclusion, selecting the right tools and technologies to support an ISMS is a critical component of preparing for TISAX® implementation. By using a SIEM system, as well as other security management tools, organizations can more effectively meet the requirements of the TISAX® standard and achieve their information security goals.

Chapter IV: Implementing TISAX®

Once you have completed the preparation phase, the next step is to implement the TISAX® standard within your organization. In this chapter, we will cover the key steps involved in implementing TISAX®, including developing and implementing policies and procedures, implementing technical controls, implementing organizational measures, and ensuring continuous monitoring and improvement.

A. Developing and implementing policies and procedures

The initial stage in TISAX® implementation is the creation and implementation of policies and procedures that are in line with the requirements of the standard. This involves defining various security policies such as access control policies, incident response policies, data protection policies, and more. It is important that these policies are relevant, practical, and effective in ensuring the security of your organization. To achieve this, it is crucial to involve stakeholders from various departments including security professionals and business users in the process of policy creation and implementation.

Once the policies have been developed, procedures must be established for their implementation and enforcement. This includes outlining the steps for implementing and monitoring the policies, and establishing processes for incident reporting, incident response, and data protection. Regular reviews and updates of policies and procedures should be conducted to maintain alignment with the TISAX® requirements and address any changes in the security landscape.

Having well-defined policies and procedures in place provides a clear framework for managing security risks, and ensures that all members of the organization are aware of their responsibilities with regards to information security. By creating and implementing effective policies and procedures, organizations can take a significant step towards meeting the requirements of TISAX® and ensuring the security of their information systems.

B. Implementing technical controls

In addition to policies and procedures, implementing TISAX® requires the implementation of technical controls that support the security of your information systems. This includes the deployment of firewalls, intrusion detection and prevention systems (IDPS), and encryption technologies, as well as the implementation of access control systems and network segmentation.

When implementing technical controls, it is important to ensure that they are properly configured and integrated with your existing security systems. You should also conduct regular vulnerability assessments and penetration tests to identify and remediate any security weaknesses.

It is also important to ensure that your technical controls are regularly monitored and updated to address new threats and vulnerabilities. This may include implementing security information and event management (SIEM) systems, which provide a centralized view of security events and alerts from multiple sources, and can be used to identify and respond to security incidents.

In addition, implementing security tools and technologies, such as security information and event management (SIEM) systems, can help automate and streamline the process of monitoring and reporting on compliance with TISAX®. For example, these systems can be used to generate reports on security incidents, vulnerabilities, and compliance status, as well as to track the implementation of security measures and the progress of security projects.

Another important aspect of technical control implementation is to ensure that the right personnel have the necessary skills and knowledge to effectively manage and maintain the security controls. This may include providing training and development opportunities for your staff, and engaging with third-party security consultants or vendors to provide additional support and expertise.

In conclusion, effective implementation of technical controls is essential to meeting the requirements of TISAX® and protecting the security of your information systems. By properly configuring, integrating, and monitoring your technical controls, and providing the necessary personnel and resources to support them, you can help ensure that your organization is fully prepared to achieve and maintain TISAX® compliance.

C. Implementing organizational measures

The TISAX® standard also requires the implementation of organizational measures to support the security of your information systems. This includes the establishment of security awareness and training programs for employees, the implementation of incident response procedures, and the development of a risk management framework.

Organizational measures are critical to the success of a TISAX® implementation, as they help to ensure that all employees are aware of their security responsibilities and that your organization is prepared to respond to security incidents.

In addition to security awareness programs, it is also important to establish incident response procedures and conduct regular incident response exercises. This will help to ensure that your organization is prepared to respond to security incidents in a timely and effective manner. The incident response procedures should be documented, communicated to all employees, and regularly reviewed and updated to ensure that they remain relevant and effective.

Risk management is also a critical component of TISAX® compliance. The standard requires organizations to implement a risk management framework that includes the identification, assessment, and treatment of risks to the confidentiality, integrity, and availability of your information systems. This requires the development of a risk management process that includes the identification of assets, the assessment of risks, and the development of risk treatment plans. The risk management framework should also include regular risk assessments and the updating of risk treatment plans as required.

In conclusion, the implementation of organizational measures is a critical step in achieving TISAX® compliance. By involving key stakeholders, establishing security awareness programs, incident response procedures, and a risk management framework, organizations can improve the security of their information systems and better protect their assets.

In addition to the implementation of technical controls and organizational measures, the TISAX® standard also requires the ongoing monitoring and assessment of your information security management system (ISMS). This includes regular internal audits, management reviews, and assessments by external auditors to ensure that your ISMS remains compliant with TISAX®. The results of these assessments should be used to identify areas for improvement and to update your ISMS as required.

Finally, it is important to maintain continuous improvement of your ISMS. This requires regular reviews of your policies and procedures, technical controls, and organizational measures to ensure that they remain relevant and effective. The results of internal and external assessments should be used to identify areas for improvement and to update your ISMS as required. Continuously improving your ISMS will help to ensure that it remains compliant with TISAX® and that your organization is better prepared to respond to evolving security threats and challenges.

D. Ensuring continuous monitoring and improvement

The final step in implementing TISAX® is to ensure continuous monitoring and improvement of your information security management system (ISMS). This involves regularly reviewing and assessing the effectiveness of your security policies, procedures, and controls, and making changes as necessary to address any weaknesses or vulnerabilities.

Continuous monitoring and improvement is an ongoing process that helps to ensure that your ISMS remains aligned with the requirements of TISAX® and the evolving security landscape. You should establish regular review cycles, such as annual security assessments and regular security audits, to monitor the effectiveness of your ISMS and identify areas for improvement.

The success of a TISAX® implementation project depends not only on the initial implementation of policies, procedures, and technical controls, but also on the ongoing monitoring and improvement of your information security management system (ISMS). Regularly reviewing and assessing the effectiveness of your security measures is crucial in ensuring that your ISMS remains aligned with the requirements of TISAX® and the evolving security landscape.

Continuous monitoring and improvement is an ongoing process that should be integrated into your organization's routine security practices. To achieve this, it is important to establish regular review cycles and establish a schedule for conducting security assessments and audits. During these assessments, you should evaluate the effectiveness of your security policies, procedures, and controls, and identify any areas for improvement. This could include updating your security policies to reflect changes in the security landscape, or making changes to your technical controls to address new vulnerabilities.

One of the key benefits of continuous monitoring and improvement is that it helps you to stay ahead of emerging security threats and respond proactively to new risks. For example, if a new security vulnerability is discovered, you can assess its impact on your organization and take steps to mitigate the risk, such as updating your technical controls or implementing new security measures. This helps to ensure that your ISMS remains up-to-date and effective in protecting your information systems from threats.

In addition to staying ahead of emerging security threats, continuous monitoring and improvement also helps you to identify and address any weaknesses in your security measures. For example, you may discover that your incident response procedures are not adequate or that your security awareness training program is not effectively communicating security best practices to your employees. By regularly reviewing and assessing the effectiveness of your security measures, you can identify these weaknesses and take steps to address them.

Finally, continuous monitoring and improvement is also critical in demonstrating your organization's commitment to security and TISAX® compliance. By regularly reviewing and assessing the effectiveness of your security measures, you can demonstrate to stakeholders, including your customers, that you are serious about protecting sensitive information and maintaining high standards of information security.

In conclusion, continuous monitoring and improvement is an essential component of TISAX® implementation and helps to ensure the ongoing effectiveness of your information security management system. By regularly reviewing and assessing the effectiveness of your security measures, you can stay ahead of emerging security threats, address weaknesses in your security measures, and demonstrate your commitment to security and TISAX® compliance.

Chapter V: Preparing for the TISAX® Assessment

The TISAX® assessment is an important step in achieving compliance with the TISAX® standard. In this chapter, we will cover the key aspects of preparing for the TISAX® assessment, including understanding the assessment scope, preparing for the assessment process, and identifying key considerations and common challenges to avoid.

A. Understanding the TISAX® assessment scope

The TISAX® assessment is designed to evaluate the security of your information systems against the requirements of the TISAX® standard. The assessment covers a range of areas, including technical security measures, organizational measures, and policies and procedures.

It is important to understand the scope of the TISAX® assessment in order to prepare effectively. You should review the TISAX® standard requirements and assess your current security posture against these requirements to identify any gaps or areas for improvement.

The assessment will cover various areas of your information security management system (ISMS), including your technical infrastructure, your security policies and procedures, and the security awareness and training programs for your employees. In addition, the assessment will also review your incident response procedures, risk management framework, and your overall security posture. Understanding the scope of the TISAX® assessment will help you to identify potential weaknesses in your ISMS and take appropriate steps to address these before the assessment begins.

It is also important to understand the TISAX® assessment methodology, which typically involves a combination of document review, interviews with key stakeholders, and on-site testing of your security controls. The objective of the assessment is to verify that your ISMS meets the requirements of the TISAX® standard, and to identify any areas where improvements can be made. The assessment team will review your policies, procedures, and technical controls to ensure that they are in compliance with TISAX® requirements, and that they are properly implemented and effectively managed.

Preparing for the TISAX® assessment requires a commitment of time and resources, but it is an important investment in the security of your information systems. By thoroughly understanding the TISAX® assessment scope and preparing in advance, you can ensure that your organization is ready to undergo the assessment and achieve TISAX® compliance.

B. Preparing for the assessment process

Preparing for the TISAX® assessment is a critical step in ensuring a successful outcome. This includes gathering the necessary documentation and evidence to demonstrate compliance with the TISAX® standard, as well as preparing for the assessment process itself.

You should appoint a TISAX® assessment team, which should include individuals from across the organization who are responsible for information security and can provide insight and evidence of your organization's security posture.

In addition to gathering the necessary documentation and evidence, it is also important to allocate sufficient resources for the TISAX® assessment process. This includes ensuring that you have enough personnel available to support the assessment, as well as budgeting for any necessary expenses, such as travel costs for assessors and any necessary software or hardware upgrades. To further prepare for the assessment, it is recommended that you conduct internal security assessments and assessments by external security experts, in order to identify any vulnerabilities or areas for improvement. These internal assessments can help you identify any gaps in your security posture and help you prioritize your efforts to achieve TISAX® compliance.

Another important aspect of preparing for the TISAX® assessment is to ensure that your organization is aware of the requirements of the standard. This includes providing training and awareness to all employees who are involved in the TISAX® assessment process, as well as communicating the requirements of the standard to other stakeholders, such as customers and partners. By communicating the requirements of the standard, you can help ensure that everyone understands the importance of TISAX® compliance and the role they play in achieving it.

Finally, it is important to establish a project plan for your TISAX® assessment, which should include milestones, timelines, and responsibilities. This project plan should be regularly reviewed and updated as necessary to ensure that you are on track to achieve TISAX® compliance. By preparing thoroughly for the TISAX® assessment, you can help ensure a successful outcome and achieve enhanced security for your information systems.

C. Key aspects to consider when preparing for the assessment

When preparing for the TISAX® assessment, there are several key aspects to consider, including:

Evidence of compliance: The assessment requires the provision of evidence to demonstrate compliance with the TISAX® standard. This includes documentation of security policies, procedures, and controls, as well as evidence of the implementation of these measures.

Technical security measures: The TISAX® assessment covers technical security measures, including firewalls, intrusion detection and prevention systems (IDPS), and encryption technologies. It is important to ensure that these measures are in place and properly configured.

Organizational measures: The assessment also covers organizational measures, including security awareness and training programs for employees, incident response procedures, and risk management frameworks. You should ensure that these measures are in place and properly implemented.

Assessment readiness: You should assess your organization's readiness for the TISAX® assessment and take steps to address any areas of weakness or vulnerability. This may involve conducting vulnerability assessments and penetration tests, as well as making any necessary changes to your security posture.

D. Common challenges and pitfalls to avoid

Preparing for the TISAX® assessment can present several challenges, including:

Lack of documentation: A lack of documentation and evidence of compliance with the TISAX® standard can be a major challenge in preparing for the assessment. It is important to ensure that all necessary documentation is in place and up-to-date.

Inadequate security measures: If your organization's security measures are inadequate or improperly configured, this can result in a failure of the TISAX® assessment. You should ensure that all technical and organizational measures are in place and properly implemented.

Insufficient preparation: Insufficient preparation for the assessment process can result in a lack of confidence and ineffective presentation of your organization's security posture. You should invest time and resources into preparing for the TISAX® assessment to ensure a successful outcome.

In conclusion, preparing for the TISAX® assessment is a critical step in achieving compliance with the TISAX® standard. By understanding the assessment scope, preparing for the assessment process, and considering key aspects and avoiding common challenges, organizations can successfully prepare for and pass the TISAX® assessment.

Chapter VI: Navigating the TISAX® Assessment

Chapter VI for TISAX® Made Easy focuses on providing guidance on how to navigate the TISAX assessment process. This chapter begins by explaining the assessment process, outlining the key stages involved, from preparation to the final report.

It then goes on to discuss the role of the assessor, highlighting the importance of having a clear understanding of the assessor's role and responsibilities. The chapter also provides an overview of key aspects to consider during the assessment, including preparing for and responding to assessor questions, documenting evidence, and preparing for the final report.

Finally, the chapter concludes with a discussion of common challenges and pitfalls to avoid during the assessment process, providing practical tips and advice on how to successfully navigate the assessment process. Whether you are a first-time TISAX assessor or have gone through the process multiple times, this chapter provides the knowledge and skills you need to navigate the TISAX assessment with confidence.

A. Understanding the Assessment Process

The TISAX® assessment process is a comprehensive evaluation of an organization's information security system. It involves a thorough evaluation of the organization's policies, procedures, and technical controls, as well as a review of its overall information security posture. The assessment process is designed to be as transparent and objective as possible and is performed by a team of certified assessors.

The TISAX® assessment process is comprised of several stages, each with its own set of objectives and outcomes. The first stage is the preparation stage, which involves the organization preparing for the assessment by gathering relevant information and conducting a gap analysis. The second stage is the assessment stage, which involves the assessor conducting a thorough review of the organization's information security system. The final stage is the reporting stage, which involves the assessor compiling a report of their findings and recommendations.

In addition to the preparation stage, assessment stage, and reporting stage, the TISAX® assessment process also includes a self-assessment, followed by a third-party assessment. This mandatory step helps to identify any gaps or areas for improvement before the third-party assessment begins. The third-party assessment can take the form of either a documentation-based plausibility check (Assessment Level 2) or a comprehensive on-site inspection (Assessment Level 3).

Upon completion of the successful audit, the final report is uploaded to the TISAX platform. The report includes the assessor's findings and recommendations, which the organization can use to improve their security posture. The successful completion of the TISAX® assessment process grants the organization a TISAX label, which serves as a third-party confirmation of their security efforts. This label can be accessed by OEMs and other partners, providing them with a verified and up-to-date view of the organization's security posture.

In summary, the TISAX® assessment process is a crucial tool for organizations looking to enhance the security of their information systems. By preparing for the assessment, conducting the assessment, and implementing the recommendations from the report, organizations can improve their security posture, achieve TISAX® compliance, and provide their partners with a clear and confident understanding of their information security system.

B. Understanding the Role of the Assessor

The assessor is the individual responsible for conducting the TISAX® assessment. They are highly trained and certified in the TISAX® standard and are tasked with evaluating the organization's information security system to determine whether it meets the requirements of the standard. The assessor is responsible for conducting a thorough review of the organization's policies, procedures, and technical controls, as well as its overall information security posture.

The assessor must be objective and impartial in their evaluation, and must adhere to the principles of confidentiality, integrity, and independence. They must also be able to effectively communicate their findings and recommendations to the organization and be able to provide guidance on how to improve the organization's information security system.

C. Key Aspects to Consider During the Assessment

The TISAX® assessment process is a complex and comprehensive evaluation of an organization's information security system. To ensure a successful assessment, it is important for the organization to be well-prepared and to understand the key aspects to consider during the assessment.

One of the key aspects to consider during the assessment is the scope of the assessment. The TISAX® assessment is designed to evaluate the entire information security system, so it is important to understand what aspects of the system will be evaluated and what will be outside the scope of the assessment.

Another important aspect to consider is the assessor's methodology. The assessor must use a consistent and objective methodology when conducting the assessment, and must be able to effectively communicate this methodology to the organization.

The organization must also be prepared to provide the assessor with all of the information and documentation that they require in order to conduct the assessment. This includes policies, procedures, and technical controls, as well as any other relevant information.

Finally, it is important for the organization to understand the role that they will play during the assessment. The organization must be able to effectively communicate with the assessor and provide them with the information and assistance that they require in order to conduct the assessment.

D. Common Challenges and Pitfalls to Avoid

As you prepare for the TISAX® assessment, it's important to be aware of the common challenges and pitfalls that organizations face during this process. Here are some of the most common obstacles you may encounter and tips for avoiding them:

Incomplete or outdated documentation: One of the most common challenges during a TISAX® assessment is having incomplete or outdated documentation. This can include policies, procedures, and technical controls. To avoid this, make sure that your documentation is up-to-date and comprehensive. This includes ensuring that all relevant documents are available, up-to-date, and reviewed regularly.

Lack of understanding of TISAX® requirements: Another common pitfall is a lack of understanding of the TISAX® standard requirements. This can lead to organizations failing to meet the required standards and result in a lower assessment score. To avoid this, make sure that you have a thorough understanding of the TISAX® standard requirements and how they apply to your organization.

Inadequate preparation: Preparing adequately for the TISAX® assessment is critical to its success. This includes having the right personnel and resources in place, as well as the right tools and technologies to support the assessment process. Make sure that you allocate enough time and resources to prepare for the assessment and that your implementation team is well-equipped to support the process.

Insufficient technical controls: Technical controls are an important aspect of TISAX® compliance and must be implemented effectively to meet the standard requirements. Make sure that your technical controls are in place and functioning correctly. This includes ensuring that your network, systems, and applications are secured and that you have the necessary tools and technologies in place to support continuous monitoring and improvement.

Lack of continuous improvement: TISAX® assessments are not a one-time event but are designed to promote continuous improvement. Make sure that you have a process in place to monitor and improve your TISAX® compliance over time. This includes regularly reviewing your policies, procedures, and technical controls to identify areas for improvement and implementing changes as needed.

By being aware of these common challenges and pitfalls, you can take steps to avoid them and ensure a successful TISAX® assessment. Having a comprehensive understanding of the TISAX® requirements, preparing adequately, and ensuring that you have the right personnel, tools, and technologies in place will help you navigate the assessment process with confidence.

Chapter VII. After the TISAX® Assessment

Chapter VII for TISAX Made Easy focuses on the critical phase of understanding and managing the results of the TISAX assessment. This chapter begins by explaining the importance of understanding the results of the assessment and provides a detailed overview of what to expect in the final report.

It then goes on to discuss how to manage non-conformities, including how to develop and implement corrective action plans to address any areas of non-compliance. The chapter also provides guidance on continuously monitoring and improving TISAX compliance, including how to develop and implement a continuous improvement plan.

Finally, the chapter concludes with a discussion of how to maintain TISAX compliance, including tips and best practices for staying on track and ensuring ongoing compliance with the TISAX standard. Whether you are just getting started with TISAX or have already undergone an assessment, this chapter provides the information and tools you need to successfully manage the results of the assessment and maintain TISAX compliance over time.

A. Understanding the Results

The results of a TISAX® assessment are an important tool for understanding your organization's level of compliance with the TISAX® standard requirements. It is important to review the results of the assessment carefully to understand both the strengths and weaknesses of your organization's TISAX® implementation.

The TISAX® assessment report provides a detailed analysis of your TISAX® compliance, including a summary of the findings and recommendations for improvement. The report may include:

Areas of strength: These are areas where your organization has demonstrated compliance with the TISAX® standard requirements. The report may highlight best practices and provide examples of effective implementation.

Areas of non-conformity: These are areas where your organization has failed to meet the TISAX® standard requirements. The report may provide recommendations for improvement, including specific steps that need to be taken to resolve the non-conformity.

Risk assessment: The TISAX® assessor may conduct a risk assessment as part of the assessment process. This is an important tool for identifying areas of risk in your organization and can help you prioritize areas for improvement.

It is important to take the results of the TISAX® assessment seriously and use them as a guide for future improvements. Your organization should develop a plan to address any non-conformities and prioritize improvements based on the level of risk and effort required. Regular assessments can help ensure that your organization remains compliant and that any issues are identified and addressed promptly.

Chapter VIII. Conclusion

The TISAX® standard is an essential requirement for organizations operating in the automotive industry, providing a comprehensive framework for securing sensitive information. The implementation of TISAX® involves a range of technical, organizational, and procedural measures to ensure that an organization is prepared to meet the demands of the standard.

A. Key Takeaways

In this guide, we have explored the key aspects of TISAX® implementation, including:

Understanding the background and requirements of TISAX®, including the assessment process and types of assessments available.

Preparing for TISAX® implementation, including conducting a gap analysis, developing a compliance roadmap, building a TISAX® implementation team, and selecting the right tools and technologies.

Implementing TISAX®, including developing and implementing policies and procedures, implementing technical controls, and ensuring continuous monitoring and improvement.

Navigating the TISAX® assessment, including understanding the assessment process, key aspects to consider, and common challenges and pitfalls to avoid.

Understanding and managing the results of the assessment, including managing non-conformities, continuously monitoring and improving, and maintaining TISAX® compliance.

By following the guidelines outlined in this guide, organizations can ensure a successful TISAX® implementation and ongoing compliance with the standard.

B. Future Outlook

The need for strong information security practices will continue to grow as the threat landscape evolves and new risks emerge. TISAX® will play a critical role in ensuring that organizations operating in the automotive industry have the necessary controls in place to protect sensitive information.

Organizations can expect to see ongoing updates and improvements to the TISAX® standard, reflecting the changing nature of the threat landscape and the need for organizations to remain vigilant and proactive in their information security practices. Regular TISAX® assessments will continue to play a key role in ensuring that organizations remain compliant and continue to improve their information security posture.

C. Final Thoughts

In conclusion, TISAX® is a vital tool for organizations operating in the automotive industry to demonstrate their commitment to information security and to protect sensitive data. The implementation of TISAX® is a complex process, requiring a range of technical, organizational, and procedural measures, but with the right approach and preparation, organizations can successfully achieve and maintain TISAX® compliance.

It is important to remember that TISAX® is not a one-time event, but rather an ongoing process of continuous improvement. Regular assessments, monitoring, and improvement are essential to maintaining TISAX® compliance and ensuring the security of sensitive information. By taking a proactive and comprehensive approach to TISAX® implementation, organizations can demonstrate their commitment to information security and ensure the trust of their stakeholders.

Chapter IX. Additional Information

A. Comparison between TISAX®, NIST, SOC 2

TISAX®, NIST, and SOC 2 are all standards and frameworks for information security and data protection. However, each one has a different focus and purpose.

TISAX®:

Origin: TISAX® was developed by the German Association of the Automotive Industry (VDA) to provide a common standard for the exchange of sensitive information between companies in the automotive sector.

Focus: TISAX® is focused on ensuring a high level of data protection and security for the exchange of sensitive information, such as product and development information, between companies in the automotive industry.

Evaluation process: TISAX® assessments are conducted by accredited evaluation bodies, and they cover a range of information security controls and processes, including data protection, access control, and incident management.

NIST:

Origin: NIST is an agency of the U.S. Department of Commerce that provides standards and guidelines for a range of industries, including information technology and cybersecurity.

Focus: NIST provides a comprehensive framework for managing and reducing cybersecurity risk, with a focus on protecting critical infrastructure and information systems from cyber threats.

Evaluation process: Organizations can use the NIST CSF to assess their cybersecurity posture and develop a plan for improving their security controls. NIST also provides detailed standards and guidelines for specific areas of information security, such as encryption, access control, and incident response.

SOC 2:

Origin: SOC 2 was developed by the American Institute of Certified Public Accountants (AICPA) as a standard for evaluating the security and privacy controls of organizations that provide cloud computing and other managed IT services.

Focus: SOC 2 provides a framework for organizations to assess and report on their security and privacy controls, with a focus on ensuring the confidentiality, integrity, and availability of customer data.

Evaluation process: SOC 2 assessments are conducted by independent auditors, and they cover a range of security and privacy controls, including access control, data protection, and incident management.

In conclusion, each of these standards provides a valuable framework for information security and data protection. TISAX® is focused on the automotive industry, NIST provides a comprehensive approach to cybersecurity, and SOC 2 focuses on the security and privacy controls of organizations that provide cloud computing and managed IT services. Organizations can use these standards to evaluate their information security posture and develop a plan for improving their controls and processes.

About The Author

Michael Kirsch

As a computer scientist with a degree in media and communications, I have been at the forefront of digitization from its early days. My journey started as a webmaster at BMW AG, where I was introduced to the world of the internet and technology. Over the years, I have gained invaluable experience and expertise in the field through my work at KPMG and Novartis, where I was introduced to the world of standards and information security.

Since then, I have made it my mission to educate and introduce small and medium-sized enterprises to the importance of information security. My experience as a specialist for information security and TISAX® at the TÜV-Süd academy and as a cybersecurity expert at the EU Commission has given me a unique perspective on the industry and its challenges.

In this guide, I bring together my years of experience and expertise to help organizations understand and implement TISAX®. I aim to provide a comprehensive and practical guide that will help organizations prepare for and navigate the TISAX® assessment process, ensuring they meet the TISAX® standard requirements and maintain compliance.

www.ingramcontent.com/pod-product-compliance
Lightning Source LLC
Chambersburg PA
CBHW052232150726

48002CB00003B/1387